CW00741988

100 incredibly irritating
things about men

Series Editor: **Lucy Dear** Written by: **Jane Purcell**

Illustration: _GWJ_

Page layout: **River Design Ltd**   Cover design: **Linley Clode**

Published by: **LAGOON BOOKS**, PO BOX 311, KT2 5QW, UK.
PO BOX 990676, Boston, MA 02199,USA.

www.thelagoongroup.com

Printed in Hong Kong

ISBN: 1904797431

© LAGOON Books, 2001 and 2004

100 incredibly irritating things about MEN

A man would rather wrestle alligators than ask for directions...

After a couple of dates, a man's grooming regime consists of quickly sniffing his armpits....

When washing up, a man will usually leave the saucepan to 'soak'. Even if the saucepan has only been used to boil water…

They don't need to wear make-up...

5

The baby crying at 3am produces the uniquely male 'nocturnal deafness syndrome'...

The only time he got your size right was with that nurse's uniform…

Their hairy feet…

A man will never put his rancid socks in the laundry basket; that's a job for the laundry fairies isn't it?

Bottom cleavage…

10

They don't understand the meaning of the word 'foreplay'...

11

Toupées. You're not just being paranoid
guys. Everybody can tell...

12

Your gynaecological check up is charmingly referred to as a '20,000 mile service'…

13

His contribution to
vacuuming is to
raise both his legs…

Men think a mammogram is something to do with musical bras…

15

The baby's nappy is full, soaking wet and she's yelling, the room smells like a farmyard, yet a man will somehow fail to notice…

Because it's the gaseous emissions from men, not cars, that are destroying the ozone layer…

17

Women have colds. Men have 'life-threatening flu'…

18

HUSBAND
OF
THE YEAR
AWARDS

Men believe that rinsing a teaspoon under the tap once a week constitutes 'sharing the housework'…

A man who takes out the garbage without being asked feels the Nobel Prize is reasonable, or even expected or deserved…

A man will mock your leg wax routine, then screech for general anesthetic after getting a splinter…

21

Whoever said 'size doesn't matter' was a man (and hung like a gerbil)...

His contribution to supper is to remind you
that his mother always made her own pasta...

23

'A quick drink with the guys' means falling up the stairs at 3am, losing control of his bladder just outside the bathroom, and slurring 'I really, really, love you,' before collapsing into a snoring heap of beer fumes...

Sitting in traffic is the perfect opportunity for a man to thoroughly pick his nose…

25

He believes that yelling at the Spanish waiter, 'Oy Pedro a beer por favor' is a commendable attempt to fit in with the locals…

26

Any movie with a semblance of a plot and a body count lower than 50 is called a 'chick movie'…

Men don't have headaches – their minor
twinge is 'almost certainly a brain tumor'…

When you can't program the video, it's down to your being a woman. When a man can't figure it out, it's because the video is a 'useless piece of junk'...

29

He will refuse to see 'one of those foreign films with subtitles'; until you remind him the lead actress spends most of the movie naked. Then he becomes Mr Culture Vulture…

Accidentally leave a toothbrush at his place and you're trying to rush him into commitment...

31

A man will either dance like a demented Mick Jagger or shuffle from foot to foot like a five-year-old who needs the bathroom...

Put four young men in a car and one of them will feel the urge to moon out of the window…

33

Because they refer to women as chicks.
Why? Because we're always picking
up worms!

34

The competitive father who can't bear to let his son win a swimming race, ever. Even though his son is three and wears water wings…

35

The man on public transport, who sits in front of you, legs akimbo, so you either have to look at his crotch or stare at the floor…

He decides to fix the broken toilet himself because 'all plumbers are crooks', then knocks a nail through a pipe, flooding the whole house…

37

Men in saunas are incapable of sitting quietly; they grunt, sigh, slap their legs, and demonstrate that even though they're in the company of other half-naked men, they're completely heterosexual…

38

On vacation, he ogles other women but becomes decidedly disapproving if you sneak a look at the local talent…

39

While you are in labor, his contribution is to remind you to breathe. He then faints…

A man is biologically incapable of walking from the shower to the bedroom, without flashing his privates at you and saying: "Whoarrrrr!"

Men with receding hairlines and ponytails.
It's not bohemian, merely tragic…

A man in a suit and carrying a mobile will shout as though he's in a force ten gale and imparting information of national importance. 'I'm on the train, I'll be home in five minutes'…

43

He wakes you up after a beer and curry extravaganza and promptly knocks you out with his nuclear breath…

Staggering home, he lets off one of his comedy farts which sets off your neighbor's car alarm...

You tell him that the very sight of him makes you puke and you're leaving the country immediately, and his response is: 'Can we still sleep together?'

A man will laugh loudly at your anti-aging moisturizer, then pinch most of it...

47

Men are secretly proud of the fact the bathroom needs to be cordoned off for three hours after one of their visits...

48

Their lack of concern over
ear wax build-up...

49

He tells you he can't stand women who wear too much makeup, then spends the evening ogling some floozy who wears more warpaint than Elizabeth Taylor...

50 His table manners would make Henry VIII blush…

51

A man will pontificate about how children's toys are just cheap electronic junk and how he used to have more fun with two sticks and a ball. Then he sulks because his five-year-old wants the *Gameboy* back…

Suggest a man takes his medical gripes to the doctor and he instantly turns into a five-year-old boy with an impending math test...

53

On vacation, he can't see that a fat, hairy beer belly, even if tanned, should never be taken out in public…

Men who argue that the pain of childbirth is 'natural'. So is the pain of a heart attack Buster. We never hear any suggestions that you 'breathe' through that...

55

Men who name their sons 'junior' after them…

56

They play air guitar…

57

The deluded Latin types who wear their shirts unbuttoned…

58

The persistent over-generosity with the cheap aftershave causing an asphyxiation radius of five miles…

59

Men never notice your new hairstyle. Or that you've lost weight, height or a limb. They might notice breast implants though…

After 10 beers, any man can convince himself he's in there with Elle McPherson. She's bound to prefer him to her rich, intelligent boyfriend...

He believes that being male bestows an instinctive understanding of DIY. 'Trust me – we don't really need this supporting wall'...

62

Police break down his door because neighbors have been complaining of a terrible smell. It's his feet…

63

Goatee beards. No you don't look like an artist, you look like a goat - hence the name…

Male squeamishness about female body hair. Women spend their lives waxing and plucking, while men have it sprouting out of their noses, ears, nipples, backs...

65

When you're chatting to friends he's convinced that his bedroom performance is being discussed. No – that's only if you're laughing as well...

Workout Man would rather die than take a few pounds off the weights. Instead he'll make macho grunting noises, lift them half an inch, and spend the next month in traction...

His idea of shared intimacy is to break wind
and hold your head under the duvet...

Men whose (at best) tenuous grasp of style deserts them completely on vacation. They humiliate you up by wearing loud Hawaiian shirts and very tight shorts in public…

69

They cannot do two things at once…

Men believe that Valentine's Day Amnesia can be forgiven with a wilting bunch of weeds from the local 7-11 garage...

Going out for an Indian meal has to become a macho display of internal stamina. Who really likes vindaloos anyway?

Men are guaranteed to wander into the bathroom, just after you've applied hair removal cream to your legs and underarms, and are walking about like a penguin...

73

They only read *Playboy* for the biting political satire. Yeah and you watch George Clooney movies for the dialogue...

74

His jeans finally jump out of the drawer and shuffle to the washing machine, in protest…

76

Men who never learn that only girls are allowed to call each other 'chicks'…

The fat, greasy bloke whose car number plate reads: STUD ONE...

78

A man's idea of gardening is to sit in one,
drinking a beer...

Men who think morning sickness is a hangover…

The rowing machine, which he buys after watching *Conan the Barbarian* - After a week it will be consigned to the garden, along with the rusting set of dumb bells, and the He Man Stairmaster…

81

Drag queens who have better legs
than us…

82

He cries at *Bambi*, and then makes you sign a blood oath not to ever tell his mates…

83

Male fashion designers who would obviously prefer to be dressing boys, so they console themselves with designing clothes that are only just big enough to fit women the size of a broom handle…

84

Men who wear trousers with the waistband up to their nipples. You're wasting your time fellas. It doesn't hide your expanding belly. It also makes you look like an overgrown *Teletubby*…

85

His choice for a cozy evening in front of the video is *Henry, Portrait of a Serial Killer* with *Reservoir Dogs* for light relief...

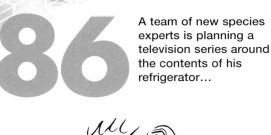

86 A team of new species experts is planning a television series around the contents of his refrigerator...

87

Mr Executive who bullies his over-worked secretary into buying his wife an anniversary present and then grumbles about the cost…

They think it's hilarious to shave off a best friend's eyebrows and chain him to a lamp post, the night before his wedding...

89

He's been boasting to his friends that you've compared sex with him to a fireworks display. Yes, but only because there's lots of noise, and it's over in three minutes…

A man will crash his car into a group of nuns, and still feel perfectly entitled to criticize your driving…

Women 'gossip'. Men hold intellectual debates on who got the most drunk last night, and the merits of Jennifer Lopez's ass versus Jennifer Aniston's…

Because men are so gullible…

Men develop a 'distinguished look' as they get older. Women go gray...

94

The only time a man will change his sheets
is when he has been sick on them…

95

Designer stubble which makes your face look as though you have an outbreak of terminal nappy rash...

96

Take a man shopping and all you hear is
'That's nice, that's nice, can we go now?'...

97

Because if he really wants a relationship with something soft, quiet and cuddly who never answers back, why doesn't he marry a cushion?

His snoring has registered 8.5 on the Richter scale…

99

They spend 2 hours in the bathroom for a simple bodily function....

Over competitive dads...